ublished by
ederation of Family
listory Societies
Publications) Ltd.
-4 Killer Street
amsbottom, Bury
ancashire BL0 9BZ,
nited Kingdom

3N 1-86006-033-1

st published 1996
printed 1999

ted and bound by
niprint,
at Clarendon Street,
ord OX2 6DP

Bas

Using

101
Family Historians

Pauline M. Litton

SERIES EDITOR
Pauline M. Litton

FEDERATION OF FAMILY HISTORY SOCIETIES

CONTENTS

INTRODUCTION

Baptism records are important as they often provide the only written record of an ancestor's early life. However, baptism has never been compulsory by law in the British Isles so, although most Christian and Jewish people were baptised at some stage in their lives, there is no guarantee that such a ceremony did take place and, even if it did, that a record of it survives. You may have to look at other types of record, such as marriage registers, census returns or Wills, to find evidence of a person's existence.

This guide outlines the various types of Baptism Record which the family historian is likely to encounter during research and in which type of record repository they can be found; some of the problems and pitfalls which may occur when consulting them; the various aids and indexes which can be utilised to locate baptisms; and books which can supply more detailed information. A* indicates that more information can be found on pages 15 and 16 of this booklet; abbreviations are given in full on first occurrence.

Note that this guide deals only with **baptism** records. Until the nineteenth century (apart from the instances on p.4) there was no requirement to register births and it was not until 1874 that registration of births became compulsory in England and Wales. See Tom Wood's *An Introduction to Civil Registration* (FFHS 1994) for details of the registration systems in various parts of the British Isles. For much of the nineteenth century, baptism records continue to be of vital importance to the family historian, either as an alternative to purchasing a birth certificate (although most baptism records — see p.6 — do not include the mother's maiden name) or because the birth was never registered.

Check in advance of a visit whether the Record Office or library in question holds the records you wish to consult, whether you need to book a seat/microform reader in advance and whether microform, printed or manuscript copies of the records are held in a repository which you can more conveniently visit. The Family History Library of the Church of Jesus Christ of Latter-day Saints (Mormons) in Salt Lake City* holds microform copies of many of the records mentioned in this booklet; its worldwide Family History Centres will either hold microform copies of the records or be able to obtain them for you to read in return for a small charge.

Many family historians like to acquire copies of baptism documents which relate to their ancestors: much depends on whether the record repository or library which holds the records possesses a reader-printer as very few repositories now photocopy originals but many will, if equipment permits, take copies from the microform. See note on Search Fees on page 14.

BAPTISMS: BASIC QUESTIONS TO ASK YOURSELF

1. **Was he/she baptised?** Most people, but by no means all, were baptised at some point in their lives. The importance attached to the ceremony of baptism varied greatly and whether and where it took place could depend on the religious persuasion of the relatives, the zeal (or otherwise) of the local clergyman, the political situation prevailing in the country, the father's occupation, the time of the year or even the weather.

2. **When was he/she baptised?** Infant baptism was the form most commonly used and the majority of children were baptised within a month of birth. However, adult baptism was not uncommon, being the norm for Baptists and some other groups. If you cannot find a baptism see **Missing Baptisms** on p.11 and **Late Baptisms** on p.12.

3. **Where was he/she baptised?** Most children were baptised in the area where their parents lived and an entry should be found in the Parish Register but, again, see **Missing Baptisms** and p.9 for possible alternatives.

4. **Will there be a written record of the baptism?** If the ceremony took place in an Anglican church after 1538 there will generally be an entry in the Parish Register and/or Bishop's Transcript but see p.6. In Scotland and Ireland many baptism registers do not commence until well into the 1700s. If the event took place in a Nonconformist place of worship the survival of a record, before the late eighteenth century, is much less certain (see pp.9-10).

5. **How much detail can I expect to find in a baptism entry?** Before the use of standard printed forms from 1813 the amount of detail included can vary widely, from merely the child's name to the full names of all four grandparents and their places of origin. From the mid-eighteenth century, occupations and places of residence within a parish may be included but are not generally given until 1813. Mother's maiden name is included by some denominations, not usually in Anglican PRs (see pp.6-8).

6. **Which sources can help me locate the baptism?** Parish Registers (PRs) and Bishops' Transcripts (BTs) (see pp.6-8); Nonconformist records (see pp.9-10); the various Indexes listed on page 13.

7. **Was there a naming pattern for children?** In England there was no set pattern although the eldest son was often named for the father (daughter for the mother). In Scotland, the eldest son was commonly named for the paternal grandfather, the second for the maternal grandfather and the third for the father; the eldest daughter named for the maternal grandmother, the second for the paternal grandmother and the third for the mother.

BIRTH AND BAPTISM

The great majority of entries in Registers in the British Isles relate to baptisms, not births. At certain times, during the Interregnum (1645-1660); and 1694-1705 and 1783-1794, when legislation ordered the keeping of lists of births for tax purposes, the number of birth entries may rise. Some incumbents always included dates of both birth and baptism but this was relatively uncommon. Occasionally an incumbent will give dates of birth only for several years but, in general, if an entry says '... was born', in the midst of the baptism entries, this may indicate a Nonconformist family (see p.9).

BAPTISM AND CHRISTENING

Many modern dictionaries treat the words baptism and christening as synonymous; older dictionaries tend to distinguish between them. The majority of incumbents similarly regarded the words as interchangeable but entries such as that in Middlewich, Cheshire *18 Dec 1801 Edward son Peter and Frances Wetenhall bapt. Mar. 5 by Rev. George Leigh and chrd. this day by Rev. William H. Heron, born 28 Feb.* demonstrate that there **was** a distinction between them, with baptism being used for the more important religious element and christening usually referring to the ceremony of public baptism (see below), which could be followed by a family celebration. Words commonly associated with the event, such as cake, gown, shawl and mug are all preceded by 'christening' and not 'baptism'. If the incumbent made one entry to cover both events, there is no problem; if separate entries were made for baptism and christening and these were several months apart, or even in different parishes, it can confuse researchers!

PRIVATE BAPTISM AND PUBLIC BAPTISM

Abstracts of these ceremonies, according to *The (1662) Book of Common Prayer* of the Church of England, can be found on the back and front covers of this booklet. Baptism mattered far more to most of our ancestors than it does to many people today because most clergymen would not permit an unbaptised person (including a new-born infant) to be buried in consecrated ground. Great efforts were therefore made to ensure that babies were baptised as soon as possible, especially if there was the likelihood that they would not survive. Baptism by a minister was preferable but, in an emergency, a private baptism could be performed by the midwife or any other "competent person". In some areas it appears that private baptisms were also carried out by the minister in the presence of the father or godparents and the child was "received into the

Congregation" (public baptism or christening) at a later date, possibly at the churching of the mother (her first public appearance at church to give thanks after child-birth). The expression "half-baptised", used in some Registers, refers to private baptism as in the example from the PR of Feltham, Middlesex: *1 Mar 1821 George William son of George and Elizabeth Turner bapt. ... said by his parents to have been half-baptised by Dr Kilgom the day after its birth — born 30 September 1817.*
Private baptisms are also common in some Nonconformist registers.

DOUBLE BAPTISMS

Most of the 'double baptisms' (two entries for the same event although often on different dates) which confuse researchers can be accounted for by one of the three situations given above or on p.12 but there are other reasons. Ask yourself:

♦ are the entries in the same parish and identical apart from the date? Date discrepancies between PR and BT, often written up by different church officials, are very common. If entries from both sources have been entered in the International Genealogical Index (IGI: see p.13) and there is **any** difference between them, they will be recorded as separate events. It is often impossible to gauge which is the correct date; reference to the original records may be helpful.

♦ are the entries for two children of the same parents? If a child died young it was common practice to give a later child the same name as the deceased infant — and, incidentally, not uncommon for the second child in later life to adopt the age and identity of the first. In some areas in the sixteenth century (and earlier) it was the practice to give a family Christian name to more than one living child to ensure its continuance.

♦ did the family class as gentry? In such families — whether Anglican, Roman Catholic, Protestant Nonconformist or Jewish — children might be baptised where they were born but later entered, as a record, in the PR of the church connected with the family seat. Remember that PRs were accepted as legal documents and succession to an estate could depend on a verifiable baptism entry.

♦ is a change of faith involved? A convert to the Roman Catholic faith, for example, would be baptised into that church as an adult even if previously baptised elsewhere as an infant; a Quaker 'marrying out' might well be baptised before an Anglican wedding.

♦ is one of the entries in May or June 1837 (England & Wales) or late 1854 (in Scotland)? Some people misunderstood the new civil registration system and were convinced that they needed a 'piece of paper' to prove their existence; if they did not have a baptism certificate they were baptised again to obtain one.

For more detailed descriptions of private and public baptism etc. see *National Index of Parish Registers,* Vol.1* or *Seeing Double: Part 1 Baptisms* in *Family Tree Magazine** Vol.4 No.4 (Feb. 1988).

BAPTISM ENTRIES IN PARISH REGISTERS

The keeping of Parish Registers for **England and Wales** commenced in 1538 but only a small number survive from this date; many begin in the seventeenth century and many early ones have been lost or destroyed so that Bishops' Transcripts (see p.8) may provide the main evidence for baptism entries in these parishes. Parish Registers in **Scotland** and **Ireland** also commenced in the sixteenth century but were less regularly kept than those in England and, generally speaking, Registers in these countries do not survive before the mid-eighteenth century, except in some urban areas. For more details see *Tracing Your British Ancestors* and other books on page 16.

The information included in Baptism Registers in all parts of the British Isles, certainly from the late eighteenth century, will usually include the date of baptism, the name of the child and its father and often the mother's Christian name but not necessarily any further information. Entries in Scottish Registers and most Roman Catholic Registers will normally give the mother's maiden name; some English Nonconformist registers also include this. Legislation governing the content of Registers in England and Wales tended to be reflected eventually in those kept elsewhere in the British Isles but the following comments mostly relate to English and Welsh Registers.

1538-1754

Some PRs include separate records of baptisms, marriages and burials in columns on the same page; others use different parts of the same book; many run all three types of event together in a chronological sequence.

Early Registers can be difficult to read, particularly in microform. Try to make sure that records are present for every year — vellum was expensive and many clerks, having left a space for whatever reason, would go back and fill it up years later, without necessarily making a note 'for 1725 go back 15 pages' as one did. Remember that spelling was of little importance to most people (illiteracy was common); when searching a PR always take regional accents into account and be prepared for particular problems with any name beginning with 'H' (which may lose it), a vowel (may collect 'H'), C or K and G or J (often interchangeable), and Mc/Mac or O' (often dropped). Also beware of mis-reading a long 's' as 'f'' (as in Hassall, read as Hafsall).

Until 1733, when English became the official language for all legal documents (including PRs), many were completely or sporadically kept in dog Latin: fortunately the words most commonly used, often in an abbreviated form, for baptism or christening are unmistakeable. *Nat(us* or *a)* [born], *fil(ius)* [son], *fil(ia)* [daughter] and *gem(elli* or *ini)* [twins] are useful to note. For a list of Latin Christian names see *NIPR* Vol.1*.

Watch for *eodem die* at the beginning of an entry — this means *the same day* and there were frequently several baptisms on one day so work backwards to the first one to locate the actual date.

Many PRs in this period contain the minimum amount of detail and baptism entries may well include the name of the child but no mention of the parents, or the statement that *a child of John Smith was bapt.* (since the fact of baptism was what mattered to the church). Many incumbents saw no need to give the mother's name! In some Registers (and, more commonly, in BTs) only the year of baptism will be given; others include the month but not the date within the month.

Between **1645-1660** many references will be to births rather than baptisms (see p.4). Be prepared for the fact that many PRs have a gap during some or all of these years. It is worth checking after 1660; some PRs include lists of retrospective entries or adult baptisms which cover this period.

c.1754-1812 From the mid-eighteenth century, with separate marriage registers being instituted in 1754, many incumbents separated baptism and burial records, using opposite ends of the same book. Some also began to include more details relating to the parents, possibly including their place of residence and the father's occupation.

From about 1770, in parts of Yorkshire, north Lancashire, Berkshire and Wiltshire (and, very occasionally, parishes elsewhere) and from 1794 in Durham and Northumberland, Registers may contain much more detail, including the full names and places of origin of all four grandparents of the child together with its position within the family. Such detail was often inserted for a few years only; your ancestor may not be included in those years but a sibling may — it is always worth checking. (Similar detail may occur in burial registers in these areas; many which omit relationships do give age and cause of death.) For further information see *Dade Registers* in *Family Tree Magazine,* Vol.11 No.9 (July 1995) and *Dade Parish Registers* in *Family History News & Digest (FFHS)* Vol.10 No.2 (September 1995).

1813 onwards

Following the passing of George Rose's Act of 1812 a standard printed form for baptism entries was introduced from 1 January 1813 and the same format is still in use in the Anglican church today. This includes columns for Date of Baptism; Child's Christian Name; Surname and Christian Names of the Parents; Abode; Quality Trade or Profession; and By whom the Ceremony was performed. Some incumbents continued to include date of birth in entries and a few recorded the mother's maiden name.

A sudden fall in the number of baptism entries in a Register may well indicate an unpopular incumbent (check neighbouring parishes), the opening of a new church or chapel or a rise in nonconformity in the area.

Bishops' Transcripts (England & Wales): in theory these are copies of the Parish Registers which, after 1597, were to be returned annually by the clergy to the Bishop, archdeacon or peculiar authority. See Volume 1 of the *National Index of Parish Registers** for more detail. Their survival rate is erratic, with some parishes having an almost complete run for three centuries and others having only a few years: see the relevant *Gibson Guide** for details of their location and availability. Remember that Cathedrals will not have BTs; some peculiar jurisdictions and liberties never returned any; and there are none for the period from c.1642-1660.

BTs are generally relatively accurate copies of the PRs but in some cases there are considerable discrepancies between the two sets of records with dates, spellings and names varying, with entries appearing in one record but not in the other and with copying errors which unite the child from one entry with the parents from another. Until England's adoption of the Gregorian calendar in 1752 (and in many parishes until much later) BTs ran from one Lady Day (25 March) to the next **or** from the annual visitation of the Bishop/archdeacon to the next Lady Day — **check that the BT runs for a full twelve months:** in some areas it is common for a gap to exist between Lady Day and a visitation in the summer. Be aware that many parishes are entered in the IGI (see p.13) from BTs not PRs. **It is always safer to check the entries in both sources.** Note that in some areas, especially before 1642, BTs survive for periods **before** the earliest surviving PR.

Illegitimacy in Registers. Most researchers will come across this problem sooner or later (see **Missing Baptisms** p.11). Entries are usually mixed with standard baptisms but, occasionally, separate records of illegitimate baptisms are found. Many words or phrases, mostly self-explanatory, are used in both Latin and English; do not assume that the term 'natural child' necessarily implies bastardy as it is often used of legitimate children. Sometimes the supposed father is named in the baptism entry; some mothers give the child the name of its father, either complete or using the surname as a Christian name. Several children baptised to a woman at regular intervals in the same parish may imply a stable relationship of a couple unable to marry. Check well beyond the last child's baptism for a marriage when a previous spouse died and be prepared for the children at this point to take the father's surname. Use of two surnames separated by 'alias' may mean illegitimacy but see p.10. Attitudes to baptising illegitimate children varied widely; some incumbents refused; Nonconformist ministers were often more tolerant; look at PRs of neighbouring churches and Nonconformist chapels.

BAPTISM ENTRIES IN NONCONFORMIST REGISTERS

The term 'Nonconformist' (or dissenter), in this booklet, covers anyone who was not a member of the (at the time) established church of the country concerned. Space does not permit more than a brief comment on records and their whereabouts for the main denominations; for more detail see *NIPR* Vols. 2 & 3*, *Understanding the History and Records of Nonconformity*, Church Registers*, My Ancestors were ...* series*, *Catholic Missions & Registers 1700-1880** and Tom Wood's articles on Nonconformity in *Family Tree Magazine** Vol.12 Nos. 8–10 (June – August 1996).

In England & Wales, the Non-Parochial Register Acts (1840 and 1857) required the deposit of Nonconformist registers with the Registrar General; those which were handed in are in the Public Record Office (PRO) in classes RG4 (1840), RG6 (Quakers) and RG8 (mostly 1857+). They have been microfilmed; most County Record Offices (CROs) and major libraries hold copies for their own counties/areas; RG4 records are included in the IGI. Some individual congregations did not comply; few RC registers (apart from some in the north-east) were handed in; Quakers complied; Jews did not. Check with the local CRO both for Registers not surrendered in 1840 or 1857 which have since been deposited and for information on the whereabouts of later records, many of which are still with the ministers but some of which have been deposited in CROs, libraries, Diocesan (Roman Catholic) or denominational archives. Year Books and Directories for the various denominations should provide contact addresses.

It is always worth checking PRs even if it is known that the family was Nonconformist – Acts in 1695 and 1705 required that Anglican incumbents be notified of births of dissenters' children (see p.4) and some nonconformists judged it prudent to register births with the established church for legal and inheritance purposes (see p.5).

Bear in mind that Nonconformist registers were often regarded as the property of the minister, not the congregation; if he moved to another area the book might go with him and some registers contain entries for congregations in several counties. Families might walk many miles to have a child baptised by a particular minister. Many ministers were responsible for a large area and a widely-scattered population so might visit outlying congregations only occasionally (causing late baptisms: see p.12).

Certain denominations, principally **Baptists** (see p.10), and **Jews,** (see p.13), practised the baptism of believers, which normally involved the baptism of adults not infants. Registers of births (especially for Quakers), or of the dedication of infants, may exist and are worth searching for.

Of the other denominations:

Roman Catholic: most baptism records begin in the late eighteenth or early nineteenth centuries, as persecution of RCs lessened and was eventually lifted. Baptism entries are usually in Latin and include names of godparents and often the mother's maiden name. Remember that with adult baptism, or at confirmation, a new Christian name may be adopted. Particularly in early PRs, the use of an 'alias' may imply a RC family, with a marriage not acknowledged by the Anglican Church. Many early Registers have been printed by the Catholic Record Society*; see *NIPR* Vol.3* and *Catholic Missions** (for list of surviving registers to 1880).

The Three Denominations [Presbyterian (inc. Unitarian), Independent (inc. Congregational) and Baptist]: in 1972 the United Reformed Church, in effect a union between the first two denominations, came into being. All three denominations have their origins in the sixteenth century but surviving early registers are scarce; Nonconformists were not obliged to keep records and some long-established chapels did not begin recording events until the nineteenth century. See *NIPR* Vol.2*. The relevant volumes in the *My Ancestors were . . .* series* list all known registers to at least 1837.

In 1742 a "General Register of the Births of Children of Protestant Dissenters of the three Denominations" was established at Dr Williams' Library; when the Registry closed in 1837 it contained some 50,000 birth registrations principally from the London area but including many from elsewhere in the British Isles and from overseas; now in the PRO in RG4 and RG5.

Methodist: Methodism originated in the 1730s but in its early years members remained within the Anglican church so baptisms continue to be found in PRs. With very few exceptions, Methodist Registers of baptisms begin only in the 1790s; in 1840, almost 1,000 Registers were handed in from the Wesleyan Methodists, Methodist New Connexion and Primitive Methodists but a sizeable number were not deposited so will not be included in RG4 or in the IGI; some will be found in CROs. See *NIPR* Vol.2* and *My Ancestors were Methodists*.

In 1818 a Metropolitan Registry was established in London by the Wesleyan Methodists for the registration of births and baptisms from the various Methodist congregations; when the office closed in 1837 it contained records of over 10,000 children; now in the PRO in RG4.

Other groups for which baptism registers survive include the Inghamites, Irvingites (Catholic Apostolic Church), Moravians, Swedenborgians (New Jerusalemites), and the so-called 'Foreign Churches', principally the Huguenots* & Walloons, and the German & Swiss Lutheran Churches (restricted to London area). See books on page 9 for more details.

MISSING BAPTISMS

In some instances it must be accepted that it will not be possible to find a baptism record for your ancestor. This may be because a person was not baptised either as a child or as an adult; the Parish Register and Bishop's Transcript for the parish where they were baptised has not survived; the family used a Nonconformist place of worship before the mid-eighteenth century and no written records were kept or have survived. In many cases, however, the record **will** survive; you may simply not be looking in the correct place. If a baptism is not where you expect it to be, note the comments on spelling on p.6, try the IGI (see p.13) and then consider the following:

- were the family nonconformists (possibly only for a short period)?

- was it the first child? The mother may have gone home to her mother for the birth and the child may be baptised in her home parish.

- was the child illegitimate (see p.8)? It may be baptised under the mother's maiden name. If the parents later married the baptism may be after the marriage or even on the same day.

- was the child baptised in a workhouse, a lying-in hospital or the Foundling Hospital (which all maintained their own baptism registers)?

- what was the father's occupation? Agricultural labourers, often hired by the year, could move from one parish to another annually. A move of a few yards could take a family across the parish and/or county boundary. Many occupations meant that couples were itinerant and children might have been baptised at any church or chapel on the canal system, along the length of a coach road, or (from the 1830s) on the railway system.

- was he in the armed forces or the militia? (check ports/garrison towns).

- did the family go overseas for a period and then return?

- at what time of year was the child born? One born in a remote area in winter, a labourer's child born in the middle of haymaking or harvesting, a soldier's child born overseas might be privately baptised but a written record might not be made until months or years later.

- did the minister write the details on a scrap of paper and lose it? In some cases it might turn up months, even years, later and be recorded in the PR but out of place, wherever the minister could find a space.

- whereabouts in the parish did the couple live in relation to the parish church and what was the geography of the area? Look at a relief map of the area — is the parish a large one including widely scattered villages; is the church over a steep hill, across a river with few bridges or miles down country lanes; is a neighbouring church close by on a 'good' road or in a market town where a baptism can be combined with business or a day's outing?

- was the person baptised with one name but known by another ("Michael Wright known as Charlie"; "Christopher Shilling known as Bob")?

LATE BAPTISMS AND MULTIPLE BAPTISMS

Late and multiple baptisms were more common than most researchers think. A separate *Ministration of Baptism to such as are of riper Years, and able to answer for themselves* was introduced into the 1662 Anglican Prayer Book (following the disruption caused by the Interregnum to the pattern of infant baptism: see p.7) and provision is made within the Public Baptism ceremony for a conditional baptism where there is any doubt concerning an earlier baptism, using the words "If thou art not already baptised, I baptize thee". In remote areas, particularly in Scotland and Ireland, parents might be dependent on occasional visits by a peripatetic minister.

Remember that:

◆ it is worth checking in the weeks before the person married: most clergymen demanded proof of baptism before performing an Anglican marriage ceremony and a baptism can sometimes be found immediately before a marriage (by licence) or some three weeks earlier (if by banns).

◆ the person may have changed his faith and been baptised as an adult — most Parish Registers will indicate this but some do not; an entry with no parents' names given may well suggest an adult baptism.

◆ whole families (sometimes including the parents) might be baptised after the birth of the youngest child; when the family settled down after a roving life (despite the fact that earlier baptisms may be discovered scattered across the country!); when a new, keen minister arrived in a parish and ascertained that many of his parishioners were not — or could not provide proof that they had been — baptised.

◆ some couples had their children baptised (perhaps years later) in the church where they themselves had married.

◆ government legislation could affect the timing of baptisms. Immediately before the introduction of a tax of 3d on baptisms, marriages and burials in October 1783, the number of baptisms in some parishes increased dramatically, only to fall sharply in the following years. When the tax was repealed in 1794 numbers rocketed again and it is obvious that many children had not been baptised in the intervening years. Similarly, in May/ June 1837 in England (with civil registration coming into effect on 1 July) and in late 1854 in Scotland some churches and Nonconformist chapels performed several hundred baptisms in a week because people misunderstood the purpose of the new legislation (see p.5).

◆ do not assume that two children in a family baptised on the same day are twins unless this is stated. If one child's baptism was overlooked, it was common practice to baptise it with the next sibling. Date of birth or age in years (and sometimes months) may be given in the PR but this is by no means always the case and the IGI (see p.13) will give only the date of baptism.

INDEXES

The International Genealogical Index (IGI): compiled by the LDS Church*, is by far the largest Index available, containing 86+ million entries of baptisms and marriages for the British Isles. This is often an easy way to find a missing baptism but **remember it is only a finding aid** and any entry found therein will need to be checked with the original source. Bear in mind that the Index is not complete as many parishes are not included and, even when a parish is represented, the entire period from 1538-1837 is not necessarily covered. If entries have been taken from the BTs there may well be gaps/missing years. Always check the Parish and Vital Records list fiche which give details of years included and the source from which entries were taken; be prepared to encounter problems as mentioned on p.6. Most non-parochial registers handed in to the Registrar-General (see p.9) are covered by the IGI: this includes the main London lying-in hospitals (p.11).

If searching **the IGI on microfiche** for a missing baptism be aware that you will need to search the set of fiche for **each** county. Bear in mind that, on the fiche, the arrangement of Christian names is strictly alphabetical, including punctuation, so if looking, for example, for a child named William check the Latin form of Gul(ielmus) together with all its abbreviations and variants and the 24 (at least) spellings of William including Will/Will./William/Willm/Willm./Wm/Wm. — a full stop can matter!

The CD-ROM version of the IGI, available at LDS Family History Centres* and some of the larger libraries and record repositories, can produce a chronological listing for any given name combining entries from all counties in the relevant country and expanding any contracted Christian names so that the problems mentioned above should not occur.

Old Parish (Parochial) Registers for Scotland: Indexes see page 14.

Quakers (Religious Society of Friends) 'Digest': before handing over their records to the Registrar General in 1840, the Quakers indexed them. This Digest (of births not baptisms) is available on microfiche at Friends' House*. Many CROs have copies of this Digest for their areas: note that the original registers include much more detailed information than this Index.

Phillimore's *Atlas and Index of Parish Registers (2nd edition 1995)* lists, by county, deposited original registers and their whereabouts.

County Record Office Guides should list indexes and transcriptions of baptism records which have been prepared for their areas — always worth enquiring. Also see the relevant *Gibson Guide*; check with the Society of Genealogists* and your local Family History Society; and look in *Family Tree Magazine* for advertisements for private indexes.

WHEREABOUTS OF BAPTISM RECORDS

There are exceptions to every rule but *in general* the following apply:

England and Wales: most Parish Registers are held in the relevant CROs, a few are still retained in the parishes but the CRO may hold a microform copy. Bishops' Transcripts for England are in Diocesan Record Offices (often, but by no means always, the CRO), those for Wales are in the National Library of Wales*. Surviving Nonconformist registers to 1837 should be in the PRO or local CRO; see pp.9-10 for more details. National Library of Wales also holds some original PRs & Nonconformist registers.

Scotland: Old Parish (Parochial) Registers [for the Established Church of Scotland] pre-1855 are in New Register House, Edinburgh* (many do not begin until the eighteenth century): indexes to these are available on microfiche in many major libraries etc. Most Registers after 1855 are with the incumbents, as are records of the Scottish Episcopal Church. There are no BTs. Most surviving Nonconformist records are in the Scottish Record Office*. **Note that there is a search fee for using New Register House.**

Ireland: for the survival and location of Church of Ireland and Roman Catholic registers see *Tracing Your Irish Ancestors*. Those for Northern Ireland are available on microfilm at PRONI*. Many registers were destroyed in 1922 but copies may survive; many do not commence until the mid-eighteenth century. There are no BTs. Presbyterian registers for the Republic of Ireland are mostly still at the churches; those for Northern Ireland are in PRONI, at the churches (with microfilm copies in PRONI) or at the Presbyterian Historical Society, Belfast BT1 6DW. For Northern Ireland, a list of Methodist registers (from 1816) with dates and locations, is held by PRONI.

Channel Islands: majority of Registers are still with the clergy: no BTs.

Isle of Man: PRs 1603-1878 are in the Manx Museum Library*, with copies at the General Registry*. Coverage of baptisms by the IGI is virtually complete.

SEARCH FEES. Note that, under the Ecclesiastical Fees Measure (1986) custodians of PRs have the right to charge fees both for consulting the register and providing copies: these fees are usually waived when the PRs are deposited in a CRO etc. but a charge (payable to the parish) may be made for the provision of photocopied entries. If the PRs are still held at the church, **check in advance** whether the statutory search fees apply (these have risen steadily from £5 an hour in 1991 to £12 an hour in 1999).

USEFUL ADDRESSES

Federation of Family History Societies (FFHS)
- **Administrator:** c/o The Benson Room, Birmingham & Midland Institute, Margaret Street, Birmingham B3 3BS
- **Publications:** 2-4 Killer St., Ramsbottom, Bury, Lancs. BL0 9BZ

Scottish Association of FHSs: 51/3 Mortonhall Rd, Edinburgh EH9 2HN

Church of Jesus Christ of Latter-day Saints:
- **Genealogical Society of Utah,** Family History Library, 35 North West Temple, Salt Lake City, Utah 84150, USA (enclose 3 IRCs or dollar bill)
- **GSU:** The Area Manager, 185 Penns Lane, Sutton Coldfield, West Midlands B76 1JU (location of Family History Centres etc. **not** research queries).

Society of Genealogists: 14 Charterhouse Buildings, Goswell Road, London EC1M 7BA

Institute of Heraldic & Genealogical Studies: Northgate, Canterbury, Kent CT1 1BA (for *Phillimore's Atlas* and *Parish Maps*)

Family Tree Magazine: 61 Great Whyte, Ramsey, Huntingdon, Cambs. PE17 1HL

Public Record Office: Ruskin Avenue, Kew, Richmond, Surrey TW9 4DU

National Library of Wales: Aberystwyth, Dyfed SY23 3BU

New Register House: Edinburgh EH1 3YT

Scottish Record Office: General Register House, Edinburgh EH1 3YY.

National Archives (Dublin): Bishop Street, Dublin 8

Public Record Office of Northern Ireland (PRONI): 66 Balmoral Avenue, Belfast BT9 6NY

Manx Museum Library: Kingswood Road, Douglas, Isle of Man

Isle of Man General Registry: Finch Road, Douglas, Isle of Man

Société Jersiaise: 9 Pier Road, St Helier, Jersey

Société Guerniaise: Candie, St Peter Port, Guernsey

Catholic Record Society: 114 Mount Street, London W1X 6AX

Huguenot Society: Huguenot Library, University College, Gower Street, London WC1E 6BT

Religious Society of Friends: Friends' House, Euston Rd, London NW1 2BJ

United Reformed Church Historical Society: 86 Tavistock Place, London WC1H 9RT.

Baptist Historical Society: 4 Southampton Row, London WC1B 4A

Note: when requesting information, it is usual to enclose a stamped addressed envelope or International Reply Coupons. Bear in mind that British stamps are **not** valid on letters **from** IOM & Channel Islands.

BIBLIOGRAPHY

National Index of Parish Registers Vols.1 (General), 2 (Nonconformists), 3 (RCs; Jews; Quakers) & 12 (Scotland): D.J.Steel (SoG 1970s)

Vol. 13 (Wales) (National Library of Wales etc. 1986)

Gibson Guides: J.S.W. Gibson (FFHS):
- ***Bishops' Transcripts & Marriage Licences, Bonds & Allegations*** (4th edn. 1997)
- ***Specialist Indexes for FHs*** (with Beth Hampson, 1998)
- ***Record Offices: How to find them*** (with Pamela Peskett: 8th edn. 1998)

In & Around Record Repositories in Great Britain & Ireland: Jean Cole & Rosemary Church (FTM, 4th edition 1998)

Tracing Your British Ancestors: Colin Chapman (Lochin Publishing: 2nd edition 1996 – 6 Holywell Road, Dursley, Glos. GL11 5RS)

Tracing Your Ancestors in the Public Record Office: Amanda Bevan & Andrea Duncan (HMSO: 4th edition, 1990) (via FFHS)

Introduction to:
    Civil Registration: Tom Wood (FFHS 1994)
    Church Registers: Lilian Gibbens (FFHS 1994)

Latin Glossary for Local & Family Historians: Janet Morris (FFHS 1989)

Phillimore's Atlas and Index of Parish Registers (2nd edition 1995)

Parish Maps (Parishes in each county of Eng., Wales, Scotland): IHGS

Family Historian's Enquire Within: Pauline Saul (5th edition; FFHS 1995)

Understanding the History and Records of Nonconformity: Patrick Palgrave-Moore (Elvery-Dowers Publications: via FFHS)

My Ancestors were ... Congregationalists (Eng. & Wales); Presbyterians/ Unitarians (English); Methodists; Quakers; Baptists; Jewish: SoG 1990s.

Catholic Missions and Registers 1700-1880: Vol.1 London & Home Counties; 2 Midlands & East Anglia; 3 Wales & West of England; 4 North East England; 5 North West England; 6 Scotland: Michael Gandy (1993) (via SoG)

Welsh Family History: a Guide to Research: ed. John Rowlands et al. (Association of FHSs of Wales & FFHS: 2nd edn. 1998)

Parishes, Registers & Registrars of Scotland (Scottish Assn. of FHSs 1993)

Tracing Your Scottish Ancestors: a Guide to Ancestry Research in the Scottish Record Office: Cecil Sinclair (HMSO: 1990) (via FFHS)

Tracing Your Irish Ancestors: John Grenham (1992) (via FFHS: includes details of PRs)

Parish Register Societies in some counties have published Parish Registers; several have unpublished transcripts available for personal consultation.